Fiddler Crabs and Fiddler Crab Care

A Complete Pet Owner's Guide

What do fiddler crabs eat? Essential information to keep your fiddler crabs healthy and happy in your home aquarium. Including habitat, facts, aquarium tank setup, molting, food, personality & pictures

Alex Halton

Published by ROC Publishing 2013

Foreword

Fiddler Crabs are often referred to as "mini" crabs for a good reason — they're tiny! To come upon a colony of these creatures feeding at low tide will make you think, for just an instant, that the beach itself is crawling.

At just under 2 inches (5.08 cm) fiddler crabs are indeed diminutive, but they are exceedingly well adapted for the place they occupy in their environment.

The crabs exist primarily on tiny bits of microscopic food they extract from sand, which they filter through their mouths. When the tide recedes, they get very busy combing through the wet sand, scuttling from spot to spot with their funny, sideways gait.

There are more than 90 species of these semi-aquatic crabs found around the world, but the ones most commonly kept as pets are the Mud Fiddlers and Red-Jointed Fiddlers indigenous to the eastern seaboard and Gulf Coast of the United States.

The vast majority of these pets are captured in the wild, from the very beaches and estuaries where they feed, because it's extremely difficult to breed fiddler crabs in captivity.

As a companion, a fiddler crab is hardly the kind of animal you'll pick up and pet, but he will still offer endless fascination.

Foreword

Since fiddler crabs spend their days scavenging, they're busy little creatures. In aquariums, they put their climbing skills to good use, and will escape if there's no lid to keep them where they belong. They will eat virtually anything, and are amazingly adept at picking food apart with their claws.

Although their eyes are actually run out on stalks from their "forehead," a fiddler crab appears to be gazing at the word with an alert expression.

Males in particular put on quite a show, waving about their one over-sized claw, and at times seeming to literally shake the appendage to make a conversational point.

Because fiddler crabs must be able to get out of the water, they require habitats that include "beaches," which leads to an unusual degree of creativity on the part of their keepers.

Some aquarists house fiddlers with fish, which can work if the right species is chosen, but the crabs need brackish water (with some degree of salt) or they will die within a month.

These interesting little creatures, if housed appropriately, do not require a high level of maintenance and are fascinating pets for enthusiasts with any level of expertise.

Acknowledgements

Thank you Heidi and Pippa for keeping me company during the long hours writing this book, also for supporting me in my interest of these very unique and amusing creatures.

Table of Contents

Table of Contents

Table of Contents

Table of Contents

Chapter 1 – An Introduction to Fiddler Crabs

Fiddler crabs, although often sold in pet stores as freshwater creatures, are marine animals that live in brackish marshes and tidal pools along ocean coastlines. Their name derives from a peculiarity of their feeding behavior.

The male crabs have a single, over-sized claw. When they feed, they use the smaller claw to bring food to their mouths. Its motion across the big claw looks like a bow being drawn over a fiddle. (Female fiddler crabs have two small claws.)

Fiddler crabs are crustaceans of the phylum arthropoda, which also contains shrimp, crayfish, lobsters, and even insects. Without access to humidity and damp ground or water, fiddler crabs will literally dry out and die.

Fiddler Crab Anatomy

Basic Fiddler Crab Anatomy

Males have one large cheliped or claw. Both claws in females are small.

Eyes on eye stalks.

Each claw has one movable finger.

Four pairs of legs.

Fiddler crabs grow to a maximum size of just under 2 inches (5.08 cm). They are crustaceans in the phylum arthropoda.

All crabs have a total of 5 pairs of legs, including the chelipeds or "claws." There are three sets of walking legs, and one pair for swimming. A tough, rigid "skin" or exoskeleton of chitin covers their bodies, which are only exposed during ecdysis or molting.

When the creatures lose their shells, the process temporarily reveals a translucent and very fragile body.

Chapter 1 – An Introduction to Fiddler Crabs

Over the course of a few hours, the crab absorbs water to increase its body size by 10-20%. The new exoskeleton hardens over this enlarged space, and then the crab will begin to grow to fill up its new shell.

When kept as pets, any crustacean's living conditions will affect the creature's ability to molt successfully. Improper conditions can, sadly, lead to tragic results.

Fiddler crabs who are unwell or nearing the end of their lifespan may not be able to molt at all. In either case, if the crab becomes trapped in its own shell, there is little you can do to help the creature.

In severe cases, the crab essentially explodes inside its shell and becomes septic as infectious agents invade the soft inner body, ultimately leading to death.

Abnormal molting or the inability to molt can also be due to stress in the environment, both inside and outside the tank, or from the introduction of toxic food or materials in the tank.

One reason hard, BPA-free plastics are recommended as tank decorations is because wood can leach unhealthy chemicals into the closed environment, disrupting the quality of the water and causing crabs to sicken and die.

When molting occurs naturally, the crab's outer shell is its most powerful protection. By design, the shell, or carapace, allows the crab to draw its legs inside as a protection against predators.

It also provides partial protection for the eye stalks, antennae, and mouth at the front of the body.

On the sides of a crab's body cavity there are two gill structures that must be kept wet. A crab can live out of the water. In fact fiddler crabs kept in aquariums have to have a "beach," but the gills cannot process oxygen unless they are wet.

Escape is the leading causes of death in fiddler crabs kept as pets. They get out of the tank, away from a source of water, dry out, and die.

Since these little guys are great escape artists, and don't realize they're likely committing suicide by doing so, a secure lid on their aquarium is a must.

Scavenging for a Living

Fiddler crabs also need mud, sand, and other aquatic sediment as a food source. As detritovores, they feed on "meiofuna," forms of life so tiny they literally occupy the spaces between individual particles of soil.

In the wild, communities of fiddler crabs live in grouped burrows in the intertidal zone. This is the portion of a shoreline that is covered when the tide is in, and exposed when the tide goes out.

During high tide, fiddler crabs pack the entrance of their burrows with sand to serve as a "lid." They remain underground until the water recedes again. They then emerge during low tide to sift through the sand for food.

The Importance of Burrows

A fiddler crab's home serves many purposes. It's a secure retreat for mating, a place to sleep away from predators, and also a refuge during winter.

These creatures are highly territorial with the burrow marking the center of the crab's perceived range of "ownership."

The burrows can reach down to a depth of approximately 24 inches (60 cm) and are usually surrounded by small, tidy balls of sediment through which the crabs have sifted looking for food. It is common to find multiple species of fiddler crabs living in the same area.

Studies conducted in Mozambique in October and November 2008 showed that fiddlers take care of their neighbors in a rather unique way.

Female fiddler crabs trade sex for protection from males in adjoining burrows. Although normal fiddler crab mating takes place underground, researchers from The Australian National University in Canberra observed some unusual behavior.

When fiddler crabs have sex above ground, it's not evidence of promiscuity, but an aspect of "defense coalitions" among territorial males and females.

Fiddler crabs are not the only animals who trade favors to gain environmental advantages. Adelie penguins in Antarctica display the same kind of bartering to obtain the best stones for nest building.

This behavior in crabs does, however, suggest a much more complex social structure than researchers once believed possible for the species.

Fiddler crabs use their burrows as secure retreats away from predators as well as a place to mate. This species is highly territorial, but it is common to find multiple species of fiddler crabs living in close proximity.

If a burrow is surrounded by small, tidy balls of sediment, it is likely occupied. Crabs sift through the sand to find microscopic bits of food, and extrude the "leftovers" as tiny balls.

At high tide, the crabs plug the entrance of the burrow and wait for the water to go back out. At low tide, they emerge again to feed.

Types of Fiddler Crabs

There are 97 species of fiddler crabs, all of which are semi-terrestrial. None reach a length of more than 2 inches / 5.08 cm. Three species indigenous to the United States are commonly kept as pets.

Almost all the specimens for sale in pet stores have been collected in the wild, since breeding fiddler crabs in captivity is extremely difficult - if not impossible.

Mud Fiddlers

Mud Fiddlers (Uca pugnax) are the most common species of fiddler crab found on the east coast. The largest population can be seen in South Carolina, but these crabs can be found from Massachusetts to Florida.

As the name implies, they prefer muddy conditions. (This variety is sometimes referred to as a Marsh Fiddler Crab.)

The most distinguishing features of this sub-species is an depression on their backs shaped like the letter "H."

Their bodies are brownish in color, but the big claw is yellow-orange or yellow-white and the long, thin eye stalks can be a striking turquoise blue. Additionally, the inside of the big claw is studded with a row of bumps.

Chapter 1 – An Introduction to Fiddler Crabs

Sand Fiddlers

Sand Fiddlers (Uca pugilator) have square, thick bodies that are white, sometimes with a yellowish cast. A male displaying himself during mating season will have a pink or purple patch in the middle of his shell.

The big claw is yellowish white and often marked by a pale orange coloration at the base, while the smaller claw is white. The eyestalks are gray.

The outer surface of the big claw does contain numerous bumps, but they are not arranged in rows and the interior surface is smooth.

This subspecies lives along the Atlantic and Gulf coasts, ranging from Massachusetts south to Florida and over into the Gulf of Mexico.

Red-Jointed Fiddlers

The Red-Jointed Fiddler (Uca minax) ranges from Massachusetts down the Atlantic coastline and around into the Gulf of Mexico as far as Texas. They are not, however, typically seen on the southern tip of Florida.

Obviously their most distinguishing features are the red markings at the articulations or joints of the big claw.

Additional Fiddler Species

Other species of fiddler crabs found along the Atlantic seaboard and the Gulf Coast of the United States include

- Panacea Sand Fiddler (Uca panacea)

These crabs are found in the Gulf of Mexico from the Florida panhandle all the way down to Mexico at the Tabasco-Campeche border. They live in sand flats and intertidal salt marshes. Their shells reach a maximum size of 0.7 inches (18 mm)

- Spined Fiddler Crab (Uca spinicarpa)

This species is distributed in the Gulf of Mexico from the Alabama coast to Tabasco, Mexico. They live in intertidal marshes and banks, preferring firmer clay and clay/sand or clay/mud soil types. Their maximum size is 0.9 inches (23 mm)

- Gulf Mud Fiddler (Uca longisignalis)

The Gulf Mud Fiddler is the most common of all fiddler crabs found in the salt marshes of Alabama and Mississippi, although they can be found from western central Florida west to Texas. They prefer salt marshes and mud to mud/sand soils. The maximum size for this species is 1.02 inches (26 mm)

- Mudflat Fiddler (Uca rapax)

The Mudflat Fiddler enjoys a wide distribution from Alabama to Texas. They are also found in the Caribbean and on the Atlantic coastline of Central and South America.

These crabs prefer moderately salty marches and mangroves where the substrate is sandy silt. Their maximum size is 0.9 inches (23 mm)

Species Similar to Fiddler Crabs

Fiddler crabs are sometimes confused with ghost or sand crabs (Ocypode quadrata) to whom they are closely related. Ghost crabs also have one over-sized claw, but not to the pronounced degree seen in fiddlers.

Ghost crabs also live on sandy shores, dig burrows, breathe through gills which they must keep moist, and release their eggs in the ocean to develop in a planktonic state. They are, however, nocturnal creatures with very pale coloring.

Ghost crabs prefer open sandy beaches and they are larger than fiddlers, often attaining a carapace size of more than 2 inches (50 mm).

Fiddler crabs also bear a resemblance to many of the crabs in the Grapsidae family. These include:

- marsh crabs
- friendly crabs
- shore crabs
- square-backed crabs
- wharf crabs

The males of these species, however, do not have an enlarged claw.

Fiddler Crabs Around the World

Tiny semi-aquatic crabs are found in many places around the world. The Acute Fiddler Crab (Uca acute), for instance, is a variety indigenous to the Indo-West Pacific and China. They are handsome crabs, with ivory colored claws, orange accents on the otherwise brown legs, and a mottled cream and brown shell.

The Typhoon Fiddler Crab (Uca typhoon) is found throughout the Northern Philippines. They are black, with alternating red and black legs.

The Elegant Fiddler Crab (Uca elegant) calls the north and northwest coasts of Australia home. Also a black crab, the big claws on males are ivory with orange accenting.

For a full list of recognized fiddler crab species with links to photographs and maps illustrating their geographic distribution, see Appendix 1:

Catching Wild Fiddler Crabs

Since almost all fiddler crabs sold as pets have been captured in the wild, and providing you are not breaking any local or regional game regulations, there is nothing to prevent a hobbyist from collecting a wild fiddler crab.

If this is your plan, however, you need to have a habitat prepared for the creature before bringing it home. Take along a bucket or container and fill it with water from the site where you will be collecting the crab.

If you will be traveling any great distance home, make sure the crab can crawl out of the water inside the container.

Use a lid! These crabs are extremely good at crawling out of almost any enclosure. If the fiddler crab dries out, it will die.

Fiddler crabs are happiest in pairs, so if possible, collect one male and one female. It isn't difficult to tell the genders apart, since all males have one over-sized claw.

As of this writing, the only endangered species of fiddler crab is the Ruby Fiddler (Uca rosea), which is listed as "threatened." It is indigenous to Singapore.

Chapter 1 – An Introduction to Fiddler Crabs

Basics of Fiddler Crab Behavior

In the wild, fiddler crabs live approximately seven years, but in captivity they rarely survive more than a year and a half.

They do not always adapt well to the artificial environment of a tank and are often characterized as "freshwater" crabs when in reality they need brackish or slightly salty water to survive.

Fiddler crabs do not have as much personality as hermit crabs, and are somewhat challenging as tank mates for fish species because they will eat anything. If a fish comes within reach of their claws and is not fast enough to get away, it will be consumed.

Male fiddler crabs have one large claw, which accounts for as much as half their body weight. They brandish the claw as if it were a weapon to threaten intruders and to protect their burrows.

That is, however, about as far as any altercation goes. A fiddler crab's idea of a "fight" is more a ritualized version of a game of "chicken." The crab that puts on the best show typically "wins," which is usually the opponent with the larger claw.

Should a fiddler crab actually lose his large claw in a fight or an accident, it will grow back (on the opposite side) the next time the creature molts or sheds his shell.

The large claw is also used to attract females during mating season, where, again, claw size equals success. In theory, the crab with the largest claw is the most attractive to members of the opposite sex. (Males also stomp their legs to make noise so potential mates will notice them.)

During the daylight hours, fiddler crabs grow darker in color, but begin to lighten at dusk. The color change not only responds to the altered quality of the light, but also to the rhythm of the tides.

Mating Behavior in the Wild

Mating season for the various species of fiddler crabs in the wild runs from June to August. The males position themselves outside the burrow and wave their large claws back and forth to attract the females.

The females walk by and if a pair takes notice of one another, the male taps the ground with his claw. If the female accepts the direct invitation, the pair go into the burrow together.

For the next fourteen days the female will then remain underground for 14 days, until she emerges with a "sponge" — a collection of fertilized eggs — on her abdomen.

She releases the eggs into the receding tide, where they will hatch as free-swimming, planktonic larvae called zoea. There, the babies go through a series of progressive molts to grow, passing through a state of life called "megalopa" before entering the final developmental generation as immature, but recognizable crabs.

At this point, they return to the land and continue to develop, ultimately reaching a maximum size of no more than 2 inches / 5.08 cm.

Needless to say, many eggs and larva are consumed by larger creatures, in particular plankton feeders, and never reach the immature phase.

Mating in Captivity

Male and female fiddler crabs kept in captivity will mate, and the female will, as nature dictates, carry her eggs for approximately two weeks to a month. Then the complications begin. When she releases the larvae into the water, it must pass through several developmental stages.

In order to survive and grow, the larvae needs a constant supply of micro-foods including plankton, green water, and rotifers. The water must be clean and stable, the salinity must be correct — and, assuming the larvae does live even a few day — you have to make certain it isn't sucked up into the filter.

The conventional wisdom holds that it is essentially impossible to successfully breed fiddler crabs in a home tank. It has been done by laboratories with extremely large "ocean" tanks, but for the hobbyist, the task is highly impractical.

Debate over Captive Breeding

Although the topic is a matter of great debate, some aquarists claim that fiddler crab larvae can be grown in a 60-70 gallon / 227-264 liter tank. It is believed, however, that the larvae actually require the motion of the waves and tide to survive.

Replicating waves in a home aquarium is daunting because of the depth needed. To create, even at scale, a 6-8 foot / 1.82-2.43 meter difference in water depth, the tank itself would need to be more than 30 feet / 9.14 meters deep.

There are "wave maker" devices that are used by serious enthusiasts, particularly those who keep reef tanks.

Chapter 1 – An Introduction to Fiddler Crabs

Although wave makers do create the visual aesthetic of ocean motion, they do so at a much more rapid rate than that which exists in nature.

A Carlson Surge Device is intended to create the effect of waves in shallow water, but often generates so many air bubbles that the tank's inhabitants are obscured. All of these devices also raise the potential for the larvae to be sucked into the given mechanism and killed.

All aquarists seek to recreate an ocean environment in their tanks to the extent that it is possible to do so, but the limitations of depth and volume simply cannot be overcome in all but the rarest cases.

When you also consider the factors of water quality, movement AND a fiddler crab's need for a "beach" in its habitat, there are too many conflicting variables for breeding this species to be a viable option.

(There are many online discussion threads where people claim to have successfully bred and raised fiddler crabs in captivity, but it should be noted that at the time of this writing, none that could be located provided photographic evidence of this fact.)

The Role of Fiddler Crabs in Ecology

Beyond being cultivated for the hobbyist and pet trade, fiddler crabs don't have a significant commercial value.

They are, however, regarded by ecologists, as an indicator of the status of their immediate environment.

Fiddler crabs are highly sensitive to contaminants, in particular insecticides. The population density of fiddler crabs in coast marshes and wetlands signals the degree of chemical presence in those areas.

Additionally, the feeding behavior of the crabs plays a role in soil aeration, thus increasing the growth of grasses by turning over nutrients in the soil.

Fishermen collect the crabs to be used as bait, especially for black drum, and fiddler crabs are a food source for other estuary-dwelling animals including wading birds, bullfrogs, raccoons, and turtles.

Chapter 2 – Fiddler Crab Care

Although hardly a pet to be cuddled or played with, fiddler crabs can be highly entertaining. Their behaviors, including claw waving, scavenging, and climbing are interesting, and, if kept properly, they are inexpensive and easily managed pets.

What to Know Before You Buy

The bulk of fiddler crab deaths in captivity not directly linked to escape occur because the creatures have been placed in the wrong kind of tank, in over-crowded conditions, and often in freshwater.

Failure to use a secure lid on the aquarium will inevitably lead to escape, followed by the crab's death, since the gills will dry out and lose their ability to process oxygen.

Fiddler crabs must have actual brackish water or some degree of salt content to survive long term. They cannot live more than a month in freshwater, no matter how pet stores may advertise them.

Males are highly territorial and will become aggressive when placed in over-crowded tanks.

Fiddler crabs are happiest in pairs, but should be kept in even numbers. Additional "odd numbered" females will be killed.

If you are entertaining ideas of breeding fiddler crabs, you may want to rethink your plan. Your chances of success are very thin, due to the manner in which these animals reproduce.

Young fiddler crabs go through an extended "planktonic" phase of development. They literally live floating in the ocean, a cycle that is all but impossible to replicate in a tank.

Making a Home For Your Fiddler Crabs

Once you have purchased your fiddler crabs, the following are the items you will need and the parameters to be followed to set up a proper aquarium environment for them.

Minimum Tank Size

At minimum, buy a 10 gallon / 37.85 liter tank to hold no more than four fiddler crabs. (The standard rule of thumb is that one fiddler crab requires one square foot / $0.092903m^2$ of space.)

The aquarium will need a solid top to preserve the correct temperature and humidly. Small tanks of this size are extremely inexpensive, and can be purchased for as little as $20 / £13.

Ideal conditions are 75-85 F / 24-29 C with a relative humidity of 75% - 85%.

Fiddler crabs need a minimum tank size of 10 gallons (37.85 liters.) That will be sufficient for four crabs.

Be sure to include a solid top. Fiddler crabs are expert escape artists. The leading cause of death in captivity for this species is escape followed by drying out. Their gills cannot process oxygen unless they are wet.

Ideal temperature: 75-88 F / 24-29 C
Humidity: 75% - 85%

Creating Brackish Water

Fiddler crabs require brackish water, which in nature occurs at points where freshwater and saltwater meet like lagoons, estuaries, coastal streams, and mangrove swamps. The salinity of brackish water changes daily in relation to the tides, so species that thrive in such environments do tend to have a high level of adaptability. Fiddler crabs cannot, however, survive in completely freshwater.

If you are planning to keep fiddler crabs only, you do not have to be as precise about the specific gravity or salinity of the water as you would be with fish. The recommended specific gravity, however, is 1.005 to 1.010.

A good recipe for beginners is to mix 2 gallons / 7.57 liters of de-chlorinated water with 2-3 tablespoons / 1.97 – 2.95 UK tablespoons of Instant Ocean marine salt (considered by enthusiasts as the leading product). Shake the water until the salt is completely dissolved.

A bag of Instant Ocean suitable to mix 50 gallons of water costs only $15 / £9 and will obviously last a very long time.

Use a submersible filter for aeration. A suitable unit would be a Duetto Submersible Power Filter, which can handle tanks of up to 20 gallons / 75.7 liters and can be purchased for as little as $15 / £9.

Physical Tank Elements

When raising fiddler crabs it's important to arrange the sand or substrate in the tank to create a "beach." The slope needs to run from approximately 1 inch / 2.54 cm at one end of the tank to 8 inches / 30.32 cm at the other. The water level should come about half way up the slope and no farther.

Fiddler crabs cannot survive unless they can climb out of the water. The sloping arrangement will also allow you to bury a plastic box or similar container in the substrate that the crabs can use as a burrow. They will need plenty of places to hide.

This arrangement will take more sand than you might think. Purchase about 20 lbs. / 9 kg to achieve the correct arrangement. The cost will be approximately $15 / £9.

It's a good idea to use large rocks at the foot of the slope to keep the sand in place. Note that when you first add the sand and water, the quality will be very murky and dirty. The tank may need a full day for the sediment to settle appropriately. Don't put the filter in the water until it is clear.

Provide a Heat or Sun Lamp

Fiddler crabs enjoy both light and heat. Even a simple plant lamp will suffice, so long as the creatures feel they are getting "sunlight." It's not necessary to buy an actual heat lamp unless you have difficulty maintaining the correct temperature in the aquarium.

Purchase two small thermometers or temperature gauges to keep an eye on tank conditions. Put one on the "land" side of the tank and the second in the water. Maintain both at a level of 75-85 F / 24-29 C.

It's a good idea, however to spend $10 / £6.50 for at least one combined unit that reads both temperature and humidity to keep an eye on that reading as well. If you choose to use a combined gauge, plan to put it at the "land" end of the tank.

To Cycle or Not To Cycle?

It is a sad fact that some people regard fiddler crabs as "throw away" pets. Regardless of their short lifespan in captivity, that attitude is cruel. Any companion animal deserves the best level of care you can provide.

Most people who keep fiddler crabs don't cycle the tank first to condition the water and prevent dangerous levels of ammonia from developing in the tank. This can be a serious mistake.

Crabs literally graze on the small organisms and plant life that live in the sand of the beaches and tide pools they call home. That microbial life takes time to develop in an artificial environment like an aquarium.

The process of cycling a tank can be lengthy, however, which is why many people don't do it. The following is an overview of basic water chemistry and the nitrogen cycle, which you will need to understand if you are planning on trying to house fiddler crabs and fish together.

Water Chemistry and the Nitrogen Cycle

Water chemistry can be an endlessly complicated topic among those who are passionate about aquaculture. Whether you are keeping tropical fish or fiddler crabs, you do have the considerable responsibility of maintaining the atmosphere in which they live. While crabs are not entirely aquatic, poor water quality will kill them.

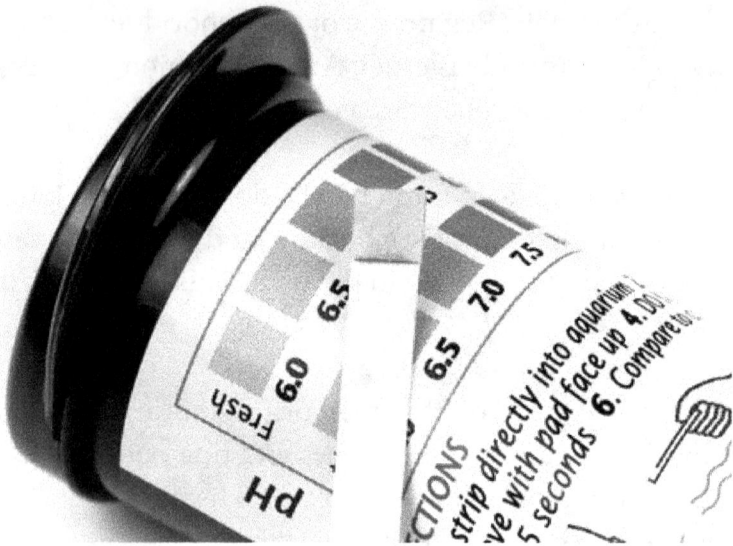

For the beginner, there are three basic measurements with which you should be familiar.

Acidity or Per Hydrogen (pH)

Typically when anyone sees the chemical sign pH they think of the associated measurement as an expression of acidity.

The actual meaning of the pH, however, is that low numbers represent more acidic water, high numbers mean more "basic" or alkaline water.

The scale runs from pH 5, which is slightly acidic to a relative neutral pH7 on to alkaline water at pH 8.

The measurement is based on the balance between hydrogen (H+) and hydroxide (OH) ions in the water.

- Saltwater has a pH range of 7.5 to 8.4
- Freshwater has a pH range of 6.5 to 7.5
- Brackish water has a pH of 7.5 or greater

Carbonate Hardness (KH)

Confusion over this measurement stems from the fact that it refers to the alkalinity of water, which is not the same measurement as "alkaline."

Alkalinity describes how well water can serve as a "buffer" to absorb and neutralize acid. High KH, water with more alkalinity, won't be subject to as many changes in pH level. In its most simplistic explanation then, high KH water is more chemically stable.

Specific Gravity (sg)

This measurement quantifies the relative salinity of water. It is taken with a hydrometer or a refractometer.

The specific gravity of natural seawater varies by location. In a saltwater aquarium, for instance, the target level would be 1.022. Once a level of specific gravity is attained in a tank, the goal is to not allow it to vary too widely.

Tanks that seek to recreate brackish waters where rivers and estuaries meet the ocean typically have an sg range of 1.002 to 1.005 sg.

Understanding the Nitrogen Cycle

Establishing the nitrogen cycle in any kind of aquarium environment is a process that cultivates bacteria in the water to keep marine species alive and healthy.
Any marine animal, including fiddler crabs, will produce waste materials that create toxic levels of ammonia in the water.

Nitrifying bacteria, however, eat ammonia, and in time produce nitrite, which, when eaten by a second set of bacteria, becomes relatively harmless nitrate.

Without this cycle, the very water that is supposed to keep your fiddler crabs and fish alive will kill them.

There are many ways to establish the nitrogen cycle in a new tank. For a beginner who intends to house only fiddler crabs, the simplest approach is to set up the tank, and then introduce household ammonia to the water.

Using an ammonia test kit, bring the water up to an ammonia level of 2-4 ppm. Then, put in a large handful of fish food. Test the water at 24 hours intervals until the ammonia levels begin to drop, signaling the presence of nitrite.

Add more ammonia to return to the water to the target range, and begin testing for both ammonia and nitrite. Add ammonia as needed and watch for a drop in nitrite.

When you have achieved 0 ppm of ammonia, 0 ppm nitrite, and get a nitrate reading, the water is ready to support life forms. Change out 70-90% of the water, and try to achieve a nitrate level of less than 40 ppm.

(This material is only a general overview of establishing the nitrogen cycle in a new tank. If you are attempting to introduce fiddler crabs into an existing aquarium, the cycle will already be in place.)

Some people do not cycle their tank before introducing fiddler crabs, but if you opt for that route, keep the tank clean and use test strips daily to watch for toxic ammonia build up.

Daily Care and Feeding

Fiddler crabs will basically eat anything you put in the tank. The crabs spend most of their time "grazing." Over time, the sand or substrate in your aquarium will be home to the microbes your pets need, but you will still have to supplement their diet daily.

The biggest consequence of overfeeding is murky, ammonia-filled water, so feed sparingly. A good daily diet would be a brine or baby shrimp or a few tropical fish flakes, alternating every few days with freeze-dried blood worms, freeze-dried plankton, and a few pieces of seaweed or algae disks.

It's perfectly fine to experiment with what you feed your fiddler crabs as long as you keep an eye on the quality of the water in the tank.

Cleaning the Tank

Maintaining proper water quality is the most important part of maintaining a fiddler crab environment if the creatures are housed alone.

Since the crabs are often referred to as "beach cleaners" and provided you don't overfeed, the creatures themselves will be very helpful in keeping their tank in good shape, even obligingly eating any algae growth.

Every six months plan on doing a total water change. As water evaporates, do not add more salt. Test the water to maintain proper salinity and only add pre-mixed water when the levels drop.

Never introduce salt directly into the tank. Remember, you can always add more salt to water, but you can't take it out.

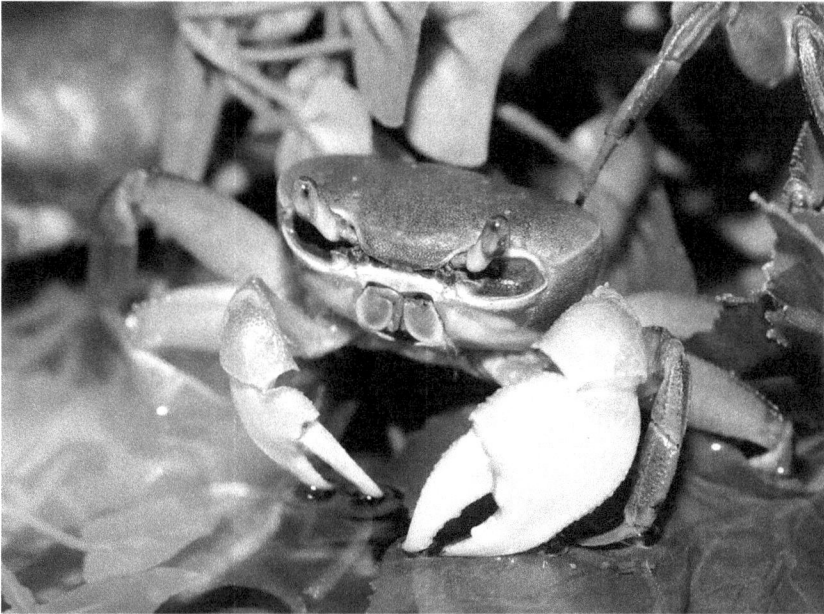

Also, only use dechlorinated water with your pets. If the crabs have left food in the tank and it is not consumed in a few hours, remove the debris.

Typically crabs will eat their own shells after molting as a source of calcium, but if they do not, take the old exoskeleton out of the tank as well.

If your fiddler crabs have been introduced into an existing aquarium, follow your typical maintenance routine.

How to Choose a Healthy Crab

Since pet stores frequently sell fiddler crabs as "freshwater" creatures, try to buy your crabs as close to their delivery date at the store as possible. The less time they have spent in freshwater, the better.

Fiddler crabs are happiest in pairs. Always keep equal numbers of males and females, and don't overcrowd. Remember that this species is highly territorial.

Try to pick fiddler crabs that are active, moving about the tank, and climbing. Note that crabs that are kept in overcrowded tanks in pet stores will be more docile since these conditions seem to have an almost sedative effect.

Chapter 2 – Fiddler Crab Care

Estimated Costs

- Fiddler Crabs - $4 / £2.55 per crab

- Tank: minimum 10 gallon / 37.85 liter - $20 / £13 will hold four crabs $16 / £10.23

- One bag Instant Ocean $15 / £9.77

- Submersible power filter
sufficient to handle up to 20 gallons / 75.7 liters
$15 / £9.77

- 20 lbs / 9kg play or aquarium sand $15 / £9.77

- 2 thermometers
$10 / £6.50

- decorative items like rocks or standard aquarium structures
varies widely
budget $10-$25 / £6.50-£15.98

- plants
varies by species
budget $5-$15 / £3.19-£9.77

Estimated Total: $100-$130 / £63.95-£83.14

*If you live in a cooler climate, your tank may require a heat mat. These units are frequently used with reptiles and are

Estimated Costs

inexpensive. Expect to pay roughly $15 / £9.77. It is also possible to use an underwater aquarium heater, at a cost of approximately $30-$40 / £19-£26.

Where to Buy Online

Aqua Pamper

www.aquapamper.co.uk
£9.99

Carolina

www.carolina.com
3-pack $17.75 / £11.34

Shipping Policy - "This item contains living or perishable material and ships via 2nd Day or Overnight delivery to arrive on a date you specify during Checkout.

To ensure freshness during shipping, a Living Materials Fee may apply to orders containing these items."

Frey Scientific

www.store.schoolspecialty.com
Item # 532187
3-pack $16.50

Shipping Policy - After ordering living organisms, a pre-paid post card for each item will be sent to you so that you can receive your item when you need it.

Where to Buy Online

Simply fill out the pre-paid post card with the arrival date of a Wednesday, Thursday or Friday, and then drop the card in the mail.

Please allow 3 weeks lead-time from the time we receive your order.

Live Fish Direct

www.livefishdirect.com
(Subject to availability.)

Fun Fiddler Crab Facts

- A single colony of fiddler crabs in the wild can be made up of thousands of individuals, so many that the beach seems to be crawling alive when they feed.

- There is no predicting whether a male fiddler crabs's large claw will be on the right or left side, however, if he loses the claw, it will always grow back on the opposite side during the next molt.

- Fiddler crabs change color through the day in response to the cycle of the tides. They are at their lightest pigmentation at night.

- When the tide comes in, fiddler crabs plug up the entrances to their burrows and wait for the waters to recede. They then emerge and begin scavenging the intertidal zone for food.

- As adults, fiddler crabs are not good swimmers. These creatures are semi-aquatic. In captivity, they must have a way to get out of the water, usually on their own little private "beach."

- Fiddler crabs do breathe air from the atmosphere, but their gills have to be moist to process the oxygen.

- Escaping their enclosure and drying out away from water is the most common cause of death among pet fiddler crabs.

Fun Fiddler Crab Facts

- A male fiddler crab's claw accounts for about two-thirds of his overall body weight and is considered a status symbol in crab "culture" and mating rituals.

- Male fiddler crabs are highly skilled at playing "chicken." They wave their big claws in menacing threat displays, generally territorial in nature, but real fights are extremely rare.

- Female fiddler crabs have been found to use their charms -- and to trade sexual favors -- for the protection of neighboring males in the colony. These are the only times when a female crab mates above ground.

- Fiddler crabs in captivity are some of the best escape artists to ever be housed in an aquarium. If you don't have a lid on your tank, your fiddler will find a way to get out.

- The vast majority of fiddler crabs kept as pets are caught in the wild because it is almost impossible to breed the creatures successfully in captivity.

- Females will mate and lay eggs, but to grow to adulthood, the young crabs must spend a portion of their lives floating on the surface of the open ocean in a planktonic state.

- The mass of eggs a female fiddler crab carries on her abdomen is called a sponge.

Fun Fiddler Crab Facts

- Currently the only threatened species of fiddler crab in the world is the Ruby Fiddler found in Singapore.

- Fiddler crabs are found on all of the continents accept Antarctica.

Fun Fiddler Crab Facts

Chapter 3 – Fiddler Crabs and Tank Mates

It is almost a given that when aquarists are told something is not possible in terms of creating an environment or housing certain species together, the first thing they will do is try it anyway.

Fiddler crabs do best living in equal pairs in crab-only environments divided equally among wet and "beach" segments. That fact does not, however, stop enthusiasts from introducing fish to a crab environment or crabs to a fish environment.

The results, generally speaking, are often predictable.

- If fish are placed in a tank with a colony of fiddler crabs, the crabs think they've been given a snack.

- If a fiddler crab is plunked into an aquarium, he's the odd "man" out.

- If the tank is freshwater he'll be dead in a month.

- If there's no way to get out of the water? Same result.

- No lid on the tank? Same result.

If you are determined to house fiddler crabs and other species in any kind of environment, you have to plan ahead and know what you're doing.

Chapter 3 – Fiddler Crabs and Tank Mates

Go with the biggest tank you can possibly afford and make sure the fish have enough water and the crabs have enough dry land.

(Note that there are some creative products and methods for creating underwater "islands" for fiddler crabs. See: Atlantis Under Water Islands at www.crabhomes.com for an example. Also see the Relevant Websites section at the back of this book for a "do it yourself" approach" to the same concept.)

Considerations of Bioload

The simplest explanation of bioload is this: how many creatures can I put in that aquarium and expect them to live? Overcrowding is a sure recipe for disaster.

When populating a freshwater aquarium, the generally accepted formula is 1 inch / 2.54 cm of fish per one gallon / 3.79 liters of water.

Fiddler crabs, on the other hand, require one square foot / 0.092903 m^2 of space per crab.

Reconciling the two calculations can be extremely difficult. The best solution is to cut the fish calculation in half if you plan to house fiddler crabs in the same environment.

If you are using a 10 gallon / 37.85 liter aquarium, therefore, you should be able to accommodate a pair of fiddler crabs and roughly five inches / 12.7 cm of fish.

Fiddler Crabs as Neighbors

Fiddler crabs will eat anything. If a fish is slow enough, or silly enough to get too close, or determined to simply mess with a fiddler crab, he will wind up on the lunch menu.

That being said, if you pay careful consideration to the use of vertical space in the tank, you will have better luck.

Anything that lives on the bottom of the tank, like Plecos, Corys, and any type of algae eater are a "no go."

Since crabs are also benthic — mainly bottom dwelling when they are in the water — these slow moving bottom feeders don't stand a chance.

You also want to avoid anything with long, flowing fins and tails, like goldfish and betas. The latter are also problematic because they're called fighting fish for a reason. An aggressive beta could seriously harm a fiddler crab if it chose to do so.

Use the following guides to pick or exclude tank mates for your fiddler crabs, including other crustaceans and plants.

Chapter 3 – Fiddler Crabs and Tank Mates

Guide: Fish Compatible with Fiddler Crabs

Unfortunately, the list of fish that can be housed with fiddler crabs is fairly small. It's difficult to find the correct balance between behavior and utilization of vertical tank space to keep all parties concerned safe.

You want to select fish that will stay in the upper half of the tank, or that are fast enough to get away from the fiddler crab. Any fish that will intentionally "mess" with the crab for the sake of entertainment are taking their lives in their own "hands."

Zebra Danios

Zebra Danios are likely your best bet as roomies for your fiddler crabs.

Danios tend to stay in the top two-thirds of a tank, safely out of reach of anything on the bottom. Remember that although your fiddler crab has to be able to get out of the water, when it's in the tank it stays on the bottom.

Zebra Danios also congregate in schools and have a "follow the leader" mentality. If one swerves to avoid a claw swipe, they all will, enhancing their chances of survival.

Given the importance of maintaining the correct bioload in the tank, go for a school of about five Danios. In stocking any tank, err on the side of less is more.

Any Variety of Tetra

Any of the various types of Tetras are also a good choice because they are very fast. They are also brightly colored fish, and add a pleasing aesthetic element to your tank.

The fish pictured above is a neon tetra and is one of the more striking of this variety of tropical tank dweller. With their vibrant red tails and iridescent blue bodies, they flash through the tank in tight schools adding high visual impact to any environment.

Guide: Fish Compatible with Fiddler Crabs

On a whole, Tetras are more inquisitive than Danios and may approach and even nip at a fiddler crab, but they're also agile enough to get out of the way of any attack.

Remember that Tetras are schooling fish, so you will want a tank with sufficient room for them to swim. This can be difficult due to the need to build a beach for your fiddler crab, so if you are going to opt for tetras, make sure your tank is large.

Tiger Barbs and Cherry Barbs

Tiger Barbs and Cherry Barbs should be able to cohabitate with fiddler crabs, but both of these fish are much more

sensitive to water quality. The crab may not get them, but poor chemical levels in the water will kill Barbs quickly.

All this being said, you will be dealing with individual fish and individual crabs. Some aquarists report that their fiddler crabs pay no attention to the fish swimming around them.

If you're lucky enough to have a crab in that frame of mind, you won't have population management issues.

Guide: Fish Compatible with Fiddler Crabs

If, however, your crab is interested then it can wreak fish havoc in very short order.

Guide: Fish Incompatible with Fiddler Crabs

This is a much longer list for good reasons:

- Goldfish are too slow, offer too many flowing fins for grabbing, and are exceedingly dirty fish, making tank maintenance a real pain.

- Betas also make for good targets with their long tails and fins, plus they can be sufficiently aggressive to injure a fiddler crab so that neither side will emerge in good shape from a confrontation.

- Gouramis are too slow, and their floating behavior practically paints a target on their side. They also swim up and down the full vertical range of the tank, which puts them solidly in harm's way of a claw swipe.

  Additionally, Gouramis spook easily, which sends them fleeing into the very hiding spots that the crabs themselves favor.

- Any kind of bottom feeder or algae eater is completely out because they are slow and live on the same level of the tank (the bottom) with the crabs, which also makes them prime targets for snacking.

- Cichlids are simply too aggressive and will stress fiddler crabs to death, while likely sustaining torn fins and potentially more serious injuries in the process.

- Puffer fish and fiddler crabs categorically do NOT mix. The puffers will kill the crabs, and have entirely too much fun doing it.

Guide: Fiddler Crabs and Invertebrates

This is also a combination that doesn't work. Fiddler crabs are highly territorial. Either shrimp or crayfish will not only be seen as food, but as interlopers in the crab's space.

Again, assume that anything that lives primarily on the bottom of the tank is out as a potential roommate for your fiddler crab. You'll be doing nothing but setting up a conflict zone if you try this combination.

Guide: Using Live Plants

Managing fiddler crabs with live plants is a chore for the simple reason — again — that fiddler crabs will eat anything! If the crabs don't eat the plants, they will uproot them and knock them over so that you're constantly having to re-arrange the environment.

Floating live plants are likely the best option given these factors.

Since some of these plants have to be acclimated to brackish water, it's best to introduce salt slowly to their environment, potentially in another tank, before transferring them to the aquarium with your fiddler crabs or fish.

Guide: Using Live Plants

The best choices in this genre of vegetation include:

- Anacharis (Egeria densa)

Although technically a stem plant, Anacharis will grow as a floating plant. It proliferates quickly. Depending on lighting conditions, Anacharis can grow as much as 2 inches / 5.08 cm per week.

You will definitely have to keep this plant trimmed back so it won't take over the tank. Optimal growing conditions are a temperature of 50-83 F / 10-28 C and a pH of 5.0-7.5.

Cost: $2.69 / £1.72

- Hornwort or Coontail (Ceratophyllum demersum)

This is one of the most popular of all aquarium plants due to its adaptability to a wide range of tank conditions. It will grow quite well floating, and thrives in temperatures of 60-86 F / 15-30 C and a pH of 6-9.

Cost: $2.99 / £1.91

- Vallisneria (Vallisneria spp.)

There are several types of Vallisneria including Italian, Contortion, Corkscrew, Jungle, and Leopard. It is also known as eel grass, tape grass, or valois.

Guide: Using Live Plants

There are both male and female plants, with the females floating on the surface. Because it is fast growing, your stand of Vallisneria will usually stay ahead of your crabs ability to keep it mowed down. It will grow best in a temperature range of 60-86 F / 15-30 C with a pH of 6-9.

Cost: $6.99 / £4.47 for 10-12 plants

- Water Sprite or Indian Fern (Ceratopteris thalicroide)

Water Sprite grows well as a floating plant and has a pleasing, lacy like appearance. This is considered one of the best starter plants for aquarists and will thrive at temperatures of 68-82 F / 20-28 C in a pH range of 5.5-6.5.

Cost: $2.99 / £1.91

- Chain Sword Plant (Echinoderms tenelus)

A prolific plant with grass-like leaves, the Chain Sword Plant grows best at temperatures of 68-84 F / 20-29 C in a pH range of 6.2-7.5. Note that this plant does need plenty of light to do well.

Cost: $13.99 / £8.94 for 10-12 plants

- Yellow Cabomba or Giant Cabomba (Cabomba aquatica)

Guide: Using Live Plants

An attractive plant with feathery, fine leaves, Cabomba does require good water quality, but it will do well as a floating plant.

It can be difficult to keep over the long run and will have to be gradually acclimated to a brackish tank. Cabomba grows best in temperatures of 75-82 F / 24-28 C with a pH of 6.5-7.

Cost: $2.89 / £1.84

- Dwarf Sagittaria (Sagittaria subulatte)

Another grasslike plant requiring only moderate care, Sagitarria should do fine as a floater, but fiddler crabs may snack on the runners it puts out to propagate. Sagittaria needs temperatures in a range of 72-82 F / 22-28 C

Note that some fish are plant eaters as well and can decimate floating plants. Any time you're populating a tank, you have to consider the feeding habits of the entire population and plan accordingly.

Guide: Dedicated Crab Tanks Reconsidered

Although it may seem like a boring idea at first, housing a pair of fiddler crabs in a dedicated environment does not have to be visually or intellectually boring.

Spend a few minutes online looking at YouTube videos of people explaining the design of their crab habitats. (We've provided some examples in our Relevant Websites section at the back of the book.)

If you are imaginative, a dedicated crab tank can be functional, easy to maintain, and interesting. Try not to adopt the attitude of a kid in a candy store when it comes to populating any aquarium environment. Often, less really is more.

Chapter 4 – Considering Crustaceans and Invertebrates

For aquarists who are attempting to create authentic replicas of underwater environments, creatures like crabs and other crustaceans as well as invertebrates are attractive to populate the tank bottom.

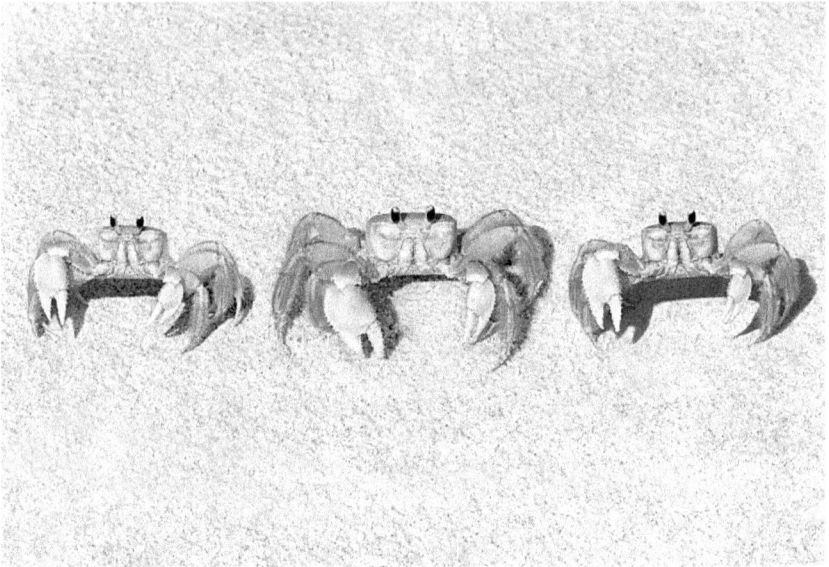

That horizontal benthic space can, however, become a battleground if it is not thought of in terms of the unique population management issues is raises.

Popular Aquarium Crustaceans

Crabs are crustaceans, aquatic and semi-aquatic creatures of the class Crustacea that have a hardened shell or carapace. This family includes crabs, lobsters, shrimp, barnacles, woodlice, copepods, and water fleas.

In saltwater aquariums, the crustaceans most typically introduced are crabs, shrimp, and barnacles. Shrimp are completely out of the question in a tank with fiddler crabs. The shrimp occupy the same lower level of the tank and the crabs will see them as just another welcome snack.

Unfortunately, the same is true of living barnacles. If dead barnacles are placed in a tank as decorations, there is also a concern because they are calcareous (mostly made of calcium carbonate). Consequently, they can harden the water and raise pH levels.

Popular Aquarium Invertebrates

Of all the invertebrates introduced into aquariums, snails are far and away the most popular. They are harmless in their relationship to other inhabitants, generally doing nothing more than gnawing on plants or opportunistically feeding on fish eggs.

Snails earn their keep, and help to maintain a tank by keeping algae growth in check. For the most part, however, snails are not tolerant of the kind of brackish water that is best for fiddler crabs. There are some exceptions, however.

The Malayan Livebearing Snail or Malaysian Trumpet Snail (Melanoides tuberculata), which grows to sizes of 1.2 inches / 3 cm, for instance, is not native to brackish water, but could live in the mildly salty water that fiddler crabs like. Unfortunately, the fiddler crabs will also like the snails — for dinner.

Keeping Aquarium Crabs

In deciding which species of crab will suit you best as a pet, try to evaluate your motivations for being interested in these unique creatures. If you simply think crabs themselves are cool and interesting, a crab-only habitat will suit you very well.

If you are hoping to add crustaceans to an existing aquarium to act as scavengers or to create a more realistic underwater / ocean shore environment, you have to consider the:

- type of water in your aquarium
- personalities of the other tank inhabitants
- potential consequences of aggression
- available space to make modifications for the crabs themselves

Fiddler crabs are semi-aquatic. They have to have a way to get out of the water. The accepted strategy for creating this opportunity is to use sand to build a beach at one end of the tank. This immediately, however, cuts in half the available space for fish and other creatures.

No matter how a pet store may advertise fiddler crabs, they are NOT freshwater creatures. At the very least you will need to introduce them to a brackish tank, which also places limitations on the kinds of fish you can raise.

Fiddler crabs are not the only kinds of crustaceans kept as pets. The other most popular variety is hermit crabs, but they are categorically not suited for life in an aquarium.

Fiddler vs. Hermit Crabs

Fiddler crabs and hermit crabs are vastly different creatures, and do not make good tank mates. Fiddler crabs are semi-aquatic, and must have access to both land and water. They are true crabs, with a shell of their own.

Hermit crabs cannot live in water, although they do require a fair amount of humidity, and they live in empty seashells they salvage on the beach. Their bodies are curved and soft, with no native protection of their own.

The tip of a hermit crabs tail is adapted to grasp the internal coiled structure of its borrowed shell. As the crab grows, it must find increasingly larger shells. Interestingly, many species of hermit crabs use "vacancy chains" when they need to move.

When a shell becomes available, a group of hermit grabs gather around it, lining up from largest to smallest. Whoever can fit, moves into the vacant shell, leaving its own shell for the next "man" down the line.

There are even instances of home invasions among hermit crabs, with several ganging up on a neighbor with a better piece of real estate. The gang pries the unsuspecting homeowner from his house and then fight over who gets to take it over.

The species of hermit crabs most commonly kept as pets are the Caribbean (Coenobita clypeatus), Australian (Coenobita variables), and Ecuadorian (Coenobita compresses.)

As pets, these interesting little house hunters are gregarious and do best in small communities. Like fiddlers, they can live quite happily in a 10 gallon / 37.85 liter tank with a layer of sand in the bottom and water in dishes for drinking and bathing.

Many enthusiasts insist the hermit crabs have more personality than fiddler crabs and are more fun to watch. They do, arguably, require less equipment and their habitats are easier to clean.

Fiddler Crabs vs. Rainbow Land Crabs (UK)

The species of land crab most commonly kept as a pet in the UK is the Rainbow Land Crab. Since they are similar to fiddler crabs, most of the advice offered in this book will apply equally well to their care.

Rainbow Land Crabs are spectacular creatures, beautifully colored in vibrant and contrasting shades. Their legs are orange, set against a bluish-black body, with purple and cream markings on their claws.

Like fiddler crabs, Rainbow Land Crabs are semi-aquatic and will require a habitat divided between a water and "beach" area. (Like fiddlers, Rainbow crabs dig burrows.)

Rainbow crabs can reach a maximum size of 7.8 inches / 20 cm across the shell, but are typically much smaller in captivity.

Since they are a solitary breed and should be housed alone, their larger size in comparison to fiddler crabs doesn't pose a significant hurdle to keeping one as a pet.

The usual 10 gallon / 37.85 liter tank serves quite well for a single crab. Because the creatures are indigenous to much warmer climates, most enthusiasts in the UK find a heat mat under the tank to be a necessity to maintain the required temperature of approximately 22 C / 72 F.

Heat mats are used commonly with reptiles and are easily obtainable. As an example, the Zoo Med ReptiTherm Under Tank Heater retails for £8.5 / $13.29.

Another option is an underwater aquarium heater. These units typically cost $30-$40 / £19-£26.

Like fiddler crabs, Rainbow crabs will eat pretty much anything since they are scavengers in the wild. Be sure to include a cuttlebone in the tank as a source of calcium.

Beyond that, plan on purchasing commercial hermit crab food, dead crickets or mealworms.

You can also give your Rainbow crabs dead fish and chunks of fruit and vegetables.

This species can stop eating almost entirely for as long as 3 months before they molt. Continue to provide food, removing uneaten bits within a few hours to prevent a build-up of mold or bacteria.

Once the Rainbow crab has molted, it will eat heartily to restore its energy.

At purchase, most Rainbow crabs are approximately 1 year of age, and will live to age 5-7 if cared for properly. Expect to pay £9.99 per crab.

Crabs for Advanced Marine Aquariums

If you are considering introducing crabs into an advanced marine aquarium, fiddler crabs should not be on your list. Some of the species that are appropriate include:

- Mithrax Crab

Commonly available, these algae eaters are one of the most popular of all crabs used in marine aquariums. They roam about happily, often out of sight, cleaning up the tank.

They are, however, omnivores, and will eat meat if it is available. If they grow too large, they may even catch and eat fish.

- Sally Lightfoot Crab

Also called Spray Crabs, these algae eaters are very popular among hobbyists. They will eat available meat, and have been known to consume invertebrates. They will, however, be fine in fish-only aquariums.

- Arrow Crab

Another popular species, these creatures look like a long-legged spider. They have a distinctive rostrum or snout that projects out of the front of the shell.

Arrow Crabs are carnivores and will happily eat small invertebrates and small fish. Put them only in tanks with fish that are large enough to hold their own.

- Porcelain Crab

Porcelain crabs are anomurans, not true crabs. Like hermit crabs, they have no shell of their own. They are not often seen for sale, but are sometimes found in live rock.

As filter feeders, they use special fan-like appendages to capture plankton. They do not bother any tank inhabitants, and are fine for any sort of marine tank.

- Anemone Crabs

Anemone Crabs are also filter feeders. Colorful and distinctive, in the ocean they live near anemones and do not get stung by them. They are often sold with or without anemones as single or mated pairs. If available, they will eat plankton, but do well with fish food. They do need an anemone as a host, and will thrive in any kind of marine tank.

- Coral Crabs

These small crabs live as pairs nestled among coral. It is not unusual for one to come along with live coral. They are colorful and do no harm to either the coral or other tank inhabitants. (Any unidentified crab seen eating live coral in your tank should be immediately removed.)

Afterword

Although fiddler crabs can, technically, be successfully housed in brackish aquariums, this may well be a project for the moderate to advanced aquarist. For the beginner, setting up a small, crab-only environment can be a fun, low-stress project requiring minimal equipment and only moderate levels of care.

The most important consideration is to understand that no matter what any pet store may tell you, fiddler crabs are NOT freshwater crabs.

They need a degree of salt to survive. If cared for properly (which also means a lid on the tank), your crabs will be entertaining and low-maintenance pets for several years.

Afterword

It's difficult to explain the appeal of keeping fiddler crabs as pets. There is something inherently fascinating in a creature that scuttles through life sideways, brandishing his big claw as if he were the king of the world. Bold talk for a little fellow who, at best, may grow to be 2 inches (5.08 cm) across.

In nature, fiddler crabs fulfill a fairly complex role in the health of the wetlands they inhabit, serving as indicators of the presence of toxins in the environment, and efficiently aerating the soil with their feeding behavior.

They live half in one world and half in another, requiring moisture for their gills to process oxygen, and capable of staying submerged for long periods before emerging on land.

When the tide begins to come in, they seal off their burrows and wait out the water to roll back out again. When kept as pets, they need a tank divided into water and beach sections.

While certainly not "cuddly," fiddler crabs do appear to look out on the world with an alert, quizzical expression.

Their movements, especially when feeding, are not only interesting, but occasionally comical if you've given them a large piece of "human" food, which they methodically break down to crab-sized bites.

Afterword

Perfect for a child's room (with adult supervision) or as a classroom project, fiddler crabs are convivial if not overcrowded, and are one of the most accessible of all "exotic" aquarium pets.

Afterword

Relevant Websites

General Information

Absolutely Crabulous
www.absolutely-crabulous.co.uk

The Crabstreet Journal
www.crabstreetjournal.org

Best Fiddler Crab Care
www.freewebs.com/fiddlercrabcare/

Embrace the Random
The Care and Maintenance of Fiddler Crabs
www.aquilusdomini.blogspot.co.uk/2012/08/the-care-and-maintenance-of-fiddler.html

The Fiddler Crab, Uca pugnax
www.vims.edu/~jeff/fiddler.htm

Practical Fishkeeping
Fiddler Crabs
www.practicalfishkeeping.co.uk/content.php?sid=3120

Best Fiddler Crab Tank Mates: What Fish Can Live with My Fiddler Crab?
www.voices.yahoo.com/best-fiddler-crab-tank-mates-fish-live-with-3798004.html?cat=53

Mini Crabs as Pets
www.dfs-pet-blog.com/2011/01/fiddler-crabs/

Unique Idea for Designing Your Crab Habitat

Atlantis Underwater Island
www.crabhomes.com/
Create an Underwater Dry Zone in Your Aquarium
www.lifehacker.com/5929789/create-an-underwater-dry-zone-in-your-aquarium

http://www.instructables.com/id/Under-water-Dry-zone-for-fiddler-crabs/

Videos

Fiddler Crab Waving display
www.youtube.com/watch?v=Gwet0JLuqWY
Fiddler Crabs - Filmed in Brooklyn, New York at low tide.
http://www.youtube.com/watch?v=93J5JC3JEuI

Fiddler Crab Molting
www.youtube.com/watch?v=_TihBgdoFBw

A Few Days in the Lives of My Fiddler Crabs
www.youtube.com/watch?v=qMkt2POLo_4

Making a Fiddler Crab Habitat
www.youtube.com/watch?v=QBN6atggUcw

Frequently Asked Questions

How many kinds of fiddler crabs are there?

There are roughly 97 species of semi-aquatic small crabs found around the world. There are three species indigenous to the eastern seaboard and Gulf Coast of the United States that are commonly kept as pets: Mud Fiddlers, Sand Fiddlers, Red-Jointed Fiddlers

Why are they called "fiddler" crabs?

Males of the species have one oversized claw. When they are eating, they bring food to their mouths with their smaller claw. It looks like the bow of a fiddle crossing the big claw, hence "fiddler" crab.

Are fiddler crabs freshwater animals?

No. Although they are often sold in pet stores as freshwater crabs, fiddler crabs must have brackish or slightly salty water to survive. If they are kept in freshwater, they will die within a month.

Do fiddler crabs spend all their time in the water?

No, fiddler crabs will die if they are forced to remain submerged. In setting up an environment to keep these creatures, they need a "beach" or other area where they can crawl out of the water.

What are the leading causes of death among pet fiddler crabs?

In captivity, fiddler crabs either die from aggression resulting from overcrowding, or as a result of drying out following an escape from an unsecured tank. The crabs have gill like structures on the sides of their bodies that must be moist to process oxygen; otherwise, the crab will die.

What is the minimum size aquarium for fiddler crabs?

A 10 gallons / 37.85 liter tank will hold four crabs according to the standard wisdom of one crab per one square foot / 0.092903m2 of space.

Can I put fish in with my fiddler crabs?

This is a delicate matter that we discuss fully in the text. Because fiddler crabs need a "beach," there's little room in an environment designed specifically for crabs to add fish.

If fiddler crabs are introduced into an existing aquarium, you have to give serious consideration to their tank mates. Fiddler crabs will eat anything, so if they can catch a fish, it's a goner.

Please see the section on tank mates in the text for a full explanation of how to choose "roommates" for your fiddler crabs.

Appendix 1 - World Fiddler Crab Species

For photographs and maps, see www.fiddlercrab.info

Eastern Atlantic

West African Fiddler Crab (Uca tangeri)
Southern Spain and Portugal through the west coast of
Africa, down to Angola (~16° S)

Western Atlantic

Burger's Fiddler Crab (Uca burgersi)
Mexico to Venezuela, Brazil, Caribbean and West Indies,
Southern Florida

Heaping Fiddler Crab (Uca cumulanta)
Jamaica, Colombia to Brazil

Thin-Fingered Fiddler Crab (Uca leptodactyla)
Caribbean, Brazil, Venezuela, Mexico (Yucatan), rarely in
Florida

Gulf Marsh Fiddler Crab (Uca longisignalis)
Gulf of Mexico, Yankeetown, Florida to Boca Chica, Texas

Greater Fiddler Crab (Uca major)
Panama to Venezuela, Caribbean, southern Mexico
(Veracruz to Tabasco)

Appendix 1 - World Fiddler Crab Species

Brazilian Fiddler Crab (Uca maracoani)
Venezuela (Golfo de Paria) to Brazil (Baía de Guaratuba)

Olmec Fiddler Crab (Uca marguerita)
Gulf of Mexico - Mexico (La Pesca, Tamaulipas to Rio San Pedro, Campeche)

Red-Jointed Fiddler Crab (Uca minax)
Massachusetts to Northeast Florida, Northwest Florida to Louisiana, a few scattered locations in Texas

Biting Fiddler Crab (Uca mordax)
Belize to Brazil

Gulf Coast Fiddler Crab (Uca panacea)
Northwest Florida to Mexico

Atlantic Sand Fiddler Crab (Uca pugilator)
Massachusetts to Mississippi, scattered in Texas, Bahamas

Atlantic Mud Fiddler Crab (Uca pugnax)
Massachusetts to Northwest Florida

Mudflat Fiddler Crab (Uca rapax)
Southern Florida and Texas to Brazil, West Indies, and Caribbean

Brilliant Fiddler Crab (Uca speciosa)
Florida, Yucatan, Cuba, Bahamas

Appendix 1 - World Fiddler Crab Species

Spiny-Wristed Fiddler Crab (Uca spinicarpa)
Northwest Florida to Mexico

Laguna Madre Fiddler Crab (Uca subcylindrica)
Gulf of Mexico - Texas (including a few scattered inland populations) to Northern Mexico

Atlantic Mangrove Fiddler Crab (Uca thayeri)
Florida, Caribbean and West Indies, Yucatan Peninsula to Brazil

Uruguayan Fiddler Crab (Uca uruguayensis)
Brazil (Cabo Frio) to Argentina (Mar Chiquita)

Victorian Fiddler Crab (Uca victoriana)
Brazil (Fortaleza to Bertioga)

Green-Banded Fiddler Crab (Uca virens)
Mississippi to Vera Cruz, Mexico

Atlantic Hairback Fiddler Crab (Uca vocator)
Texas to Brazil, West Indies

Eastern Pacific

Clay Fiddler Crab (Uca argillicola)
Costa Rica (Gulf of Dulce) to Colombia (Buenaventura)

Beating Fiddler Crab (Uca batuenta)
El Salvador to northern Peru

Appendix 1 - World Fiddler Crab Species

Beebe's Fiddler Crab (Uca beebei)
El Salvador to northern Peru

Narrow-Fronted Fiddler Crab (Uca brevifrons)
Panama to Mexico (southern Gulf of California)

Painted Fiddler Crab (Uca coloradensis)
Gulf of California, Mexico (Bahia San Felipe to Guaymas)

Crenulated Fiddler Crab (Uca crenulata)
California, rarely as far north as Santa Barbara to Mexico
(Nayarit)

Deichmann's Fiddler Crab (Uca deichmanni)
Costa Rica to northern Colombia

Dorothy's Fiddler Crab (Uca dorotheae)
Panama (Gulf Zone) to northern Peru

Pacific Hairback Fiddler Crab (Uca ecuadoriensis)
Mexico (Kino Bay, Sonora) to northern Peru

Festa's Fiddler Crab (Uca festae)
El Salvador to Ecuador

Galapagos Fiddler Crab (Uca galapagensis)
Columbia to Peru, Galapagos Islands (possibly Chile)

Heller's Fiddler Crab (Uca helleri)
Galapagos Islands

Appendix 1 - World Fiddler Crab Species

La Herradura Fiddler Crab (Uca herradurensis)
El Salvador to Panama (possibly Mexico)

American Red Fiddler Crab (Uca heteropleura)
El Salvador to northern Peru

Uneven Fiddler Crab (Uca inaequalis)
El Salvador to northern Peru

Distinguished Fiddler Crab (Uca insignis)
El Salvador to northern Peru

Intermediate Fiddler Crab (Uca intermedia)
Panama (Panama City) to Columbia (Buenaventura Bay)

Lateral-Handed Fiddler Crab (Uca latimanus)
Mexico (Baja California) to Ecuador

Pacific Mud Fiddler Crab (Uca limicola)
El Salvador to Panama

Necklaced Fiddler Crab (Uca monilifera)
Northern Gulf of California

Musical Fiddler Crab (Uca musica)
Gulf of California, Mexico (Nayarit to Baja California)

Aqua Fiddler Crab (Uca oerstedi)
El Salvador to Panama

Appendix 1 - World Fiddler Crab Species

Ornate Fiddler Crab (Uca ornata)
El Salvador to Northern Peru

Osa Fiddler Crab (Uca osa)
Costa Rica (Gulf of Dulce, Península de Osa)
Rock Fiddler Crab (Uca panamensis)
El Salvador to Northern Peru

Princely Fiddler Crab (Uca princeps)
Mexico to Peru

Pygmy Fiddler Crab (Uca pygmaea)
Costa Rica (Gulf of Dulce) to Colombia (Buenaventura)

Energetic Fiddler Crab (Uca saltitanta)
El Salvador to Colombia (Buenaventura)

Narrow-Fingered Fiddler Crab (Uca stenodactylus)
El Salvador to northern Chile

Styled Fiddler Crab (Uca stylifera)
El Salvador to northern Peru

Peruvian Fiddler Crab (Uca tallanica)
Ecuador (Puerto Bolivar) to Peru (Puerto Pizarro)

Slender-Legged Fiddler Crab (Uca tenuipedis)
El Salvador to northern Peru

Dancing Fiddler Crab (Uca terpsichores)
Nicaragua to northern Peru

Appendix 1 - World Fiddler Crab Species

Matted Fiddler Crab (Uca tomentosa)
El Salvador to northern Peru

Pacific Mangrove Fiddler Crab (Uca umbratila)
El Salvador to Colombia

Lesser Mexican Fiddler Crab (Uca zacae)
Mexico (Bay of Altata, Sinaloa) to Costa Rica (Golfito)

Indo West Pacific

Acute Fiddler Crab (Uca acuta)
China (Hong Kong to Fuzhou)

White-Handed Fiddler Crab (Uca albimana)
Red Sea, Gulf of Aden, Socotra, Arabian Sea, Oman, south
Gulf of Oman, southeastern and southwestern Persian Gulf,
western part of the Gulf of Oman

Ring-Legged Fiddler Crab (Uca annulipes)
Madagascar, South Africa to Somalia, India to southern
China, Philippines, Indonesia, Malaysia

Bowed Fiddler Crab (Uca arcuata)
China, Taiwan, Korea, Japan

Belligerent Fiddler Crab (Uca bellator)
Philippines, Malaysia, Indonesia

Appendix 1 - World Fiddler Crab Species

Bengal Fiddler Crab (Uca bengali)
Eastern India, Burma, Thailand, Western Malaysia, Indonesia (Sumatra)

Northern Calling Fiddler Crab (Uca borealis)
China, Taiwan

Capricorn Fiddler Crab (Uca capricornis)
Australia (Northwest coast through North coast)

Green-Eyed Fiddler Crab (Uca chlorophthalmus)
Eastern Africa - Kenya to South Africa, Madagascar

Compressed Fiddler Crab (Uca coarctata)
Australia (northeast coast), Indonesia, Philippines, New Guinea, Taiwan

Thick-Legged Fiddler Crab (Uca crassipes)
China, Japan, Philippines, Thailand, Indonesia, Papa New Guinea, Melanesia, Micronesia

Cryptic Fiddler Crab (Uca cryptica)
Indonesia, Philippines

Dampier's Fiddler Crab (Uca dampieri)
Australia (Northwest coast through North coast)

Demanding Fiddler Crab (Uca demani)
Indonesia, Southern Philippines

Appendix 1 - World Fiddler Crab Species

Dussumier's Fiddler Crab (Uca dussumieri)
China, Taiwan, Thailand, Indonesia, Northwestern
Australia, Papa New Guinea

Elegant Fiddler Crab (Uca elegans)
Australia (Northwest coast through North coast)
Flame-Backed Fiddler Crab (Uca flammula)
Australia (Northwest Coast to North Coast), New Guinea
(Western)

Forceps Fiddler Crab (Uca forcipata)
Thailand, Malaysia, Western Indonesia

Taiwanese Fiddler Crab (Uca formosensis)
Taiwan

Western Calling Fiddler Crab (Uca hesperiae)
South Africa to Somalia, Southern India, Burma, Thailand,
Western Indonesia, Western Malaysia

Hairy-Handed Fiddler Crab (Uca hirsutimanus)
Australia (North coast)

Inversed Fiddler Crab (Uca inversa)
Western Indian Ocean: Madagasca, South Africa to Red
Sea, Gulf of Aden, southern Oman (Dhofar), Persian Gulf,
Gulf of Oman

Iranian Fiddler Crab (Uca iranica)
Persian Gulf and Gulf of Oman

Appendix 1 - World Fiddler Crab Species

Jocelyn's Fiddler Crab (Uca jocelynae)
Pacific islands west of Fiji, including Japan (Ryukyus),
Taiwan, the Philippines, Indonesia, Papua New Guinea,
and Vanuatu

Milky Fiddler Crab (Uca lactea)
China, Taiwan, South Korea, Japan

Long-Fingered Fiddler Crab (Uca longidigitum)
Australia (Northeast coast)

Mjöberg's Fiddler Crab (Uca mjoebergi)
Australia (Northwest Territory to Western Australia),
scattered records on New Guinea and central Indonesia

Eastern Calling Fiddler Crab (Uca neocultrimana)
Fiji, Wallis, Samoa

Spined Fiddler Crab (Uca paradussumieri)
Northeastern India, Thailand, Indonesia, Malaysia,
Vietnam, Cambodia China

Perplexing Fiddler Crab (Uca perplexa)
Eastern Indian Ocean (from the Nicobar Islands eastward),
Thailand to China, Taiwan, Japan, Philippines, Indonesia,
Australia (east coast), Pacific islands

Polished Fiddler Crab (Uca polita)
Australia (Northwest coast through Northeast coast)

Appendix 1 - World Fiddler Crab Species

Asian Mangrove Fiddler Crab (Uca rhizophorae)
Singapore, Malaysia (Sarawak)
Rose Fiddler Crab (Uca rosea)
Western India to Malaysia, Western Indonesia

Shaking Fiddler Crab (Uca seismella)
Australia (Northwest coast through Northeast coast)

Signaling Fiddler Crab (Uca signata)
Australia (Northwest coast through Northeast coast)

Indus Fiddler Crab (Uca sindensis)
Persian Gulf, Gulf of Oman, Pakistan

Splendid Fiddler Crab (Uca splendida)
China, Vietnam, Taiwan

Tetragonal Fiddler Crab (Uca tetragonon)
South Africa to Iran, Madagascar, Thailand, Malaysia,
Australia, Indonesia, Philippines, Papa New Guinea,
Taiwan, Micronesia, Melanesia

Triangular Fiddler Crab (Uca triangularis)
Australia, Indonesia, Malaysia, Philippines, Taiwan, China,
Papa New Guinea

Typhoon Fiddler Crab (Uca typhoni)
Northern Philippines

Appendix 1 - World Fiddler Crab Species

d'Urville's Fiddler Crab (Uca urvillei)
South Africa to Tanzania, Saudi Arabia (Red Sea), Western
India, Thailand

Calling Fiddler Crab (Uca vocans)
China, Burma, Thailand, Indonesia, Philippines, Malaysia

Southern Calling Fiddler Crab (Uca vomeris)
Australia (east coast), Papa New Guinea, Melanesia

Appendix 2 - Selection of Scholarly Articles

Note: For those readers interested in a more in-depth and scientific consideration of fiddler crabs, their biology, social structure, and environmental role, we provide the following references to serve as an introduction to the vast body of scholarly literature on these fascinating creatures.

Abbott, J.F. 1913. The effect of distilled water upon the fiddler crab. Biological Bulletin 24(3):169-174.

Abele, L.G., and W. Kim. 1986. An Illustrated Guide to the Marine Decapod Crustaceans of Florida Tallahassee, FL: State of Florida Department of Environmental Regulation.

Allen, R.K. 1976. Common Intertidal Invertebrates of Southern California. Revised Edition Palo Alto, CA: Peek Publications.

Aspey, W.P. 1978. Fiddler crab behavioral ecology: Burrow density in Uca pugnax (Smith) and Uca pugilator (Bosc) (Decapoda Brachyura). Crustaceana 34(3):235-244.

Bachand, R.G. 1979. The fascinating fiddler crab. Underwater Naturalist 11(4):12-14.

Baird, J.L., Jr., and A.L. Burleson. 1970. An analysis of locomotor behavior in the fiddler crab Uca pugilator. American Zoologist 10(4):500.

Appendix 2 - Selection of Scholarly Articles

Barnwell, F.H. 1966. Daily and tidal patterns of activity in individual fiddler crab (genus Uca) from the Woods Hole region. Biological Bulletin 130(1):1-17.

Barnwell, F.H. 1968. The role of rhythmic systems in the adaptation of fiddler crabs to the intertidal zone. American Zoologist 8(3):569-583.

Barnwell, F.H., and C.L. Thurman, II. 1984. Taxonomy and biogeography of fiddler crabs (Ocypodidae: genus Uca) of the Atlantic and Gulf coasts of eastern North America. Zoological Journal of the Linnean Society 81:23-87.

Becker, J.M., and G.W. Hinsch. 1982. Structural differences in male and female burrows of Uca pugilator. Florida Scientist 45(SUPPL. 1):19.

Bell, S.S., M.C. Watzin, and B.C. Coull. 1978. Biogenic structure and its effect on the spatial heterogeneity of meiofauna in a salt marsh. Journal of Experimental Marine Biology and Ecology 35(2):99-107.

Bergey, L.L., and J.S. Weis. 2008. Aspects of population ecology in two populations of fiddler crabs, Uca pugnax. Marine Biology 154(3):435-442.

Bergin, M.E. 1981. Hatching rhythms in Uca pugilator (Decapoda: Brachyura). Marine Biology 63:151-158.

Bertness, M.D., and T. Miller. 1984. The distribution and dynamics of Uca pugnax (Smith) burrows in a New

England salt marsh. Journal of Experimental Marine Biology and Ecology 83(3):211-237.

Bliss, D.E. 1982. Shrimps, Lobsters and Crabs New York: Columbia University Press.

Bogazzi, E., O.O. Iribarne, R. Guerrero, and E.D. Spivak. 2001. Wind pattern may explain the southern limit of distribution of a southwestern Atlantic fiddler crab. Journal of Shellfish Research 20(1):353-360.

Bolton, J., S. Callander, M.D. Jennions, and P.R.Y. Backwell. 2011. Even weak males help their neighbours: Defence coalitions in a fiddler crab. Ethology 117(11):1027-1030.

Booksmythe, I., T. Detto, and P.R.Y. Backwell. 2008. Female fiddler crabs settle for less: the travel costs of mate choice. Animal Behaviour 76:1775-1781.

Booksmythe, I., R.N.C. Milner, M.D. Jennions, and P.R.Y. Backwell. 2010. How do weaponless male fiddler crabs avoid aggression? Behavioral Ecology and Sociobiology 64(3):485-491.

Bright, D.B., and C.L. Hogue. 1972. A synopsis of the burrowing land crabs of the world and list of their arthropod symbionts and burrow associates. Contributions in Science. Natural History Museum of Los Angeles County 220:1-58.

Brodie, R.J. 2004. Life on the wedge: Survival of low salinity conditions in larvae of the fiddler crab Uca minax. Integrative and Comparative Biology 44(6):530.

Brown, S.K., and R.E. Loveland. 1980. Reproductive cycles of the fiddler crabs Uca minax and Uca pugnax. American Zoologist 20:957.

Brusca, R.C. 1980. Common Intertidal Invertebrates of the Gulf of California. Second Edition Tucson, Arizona: University of Arizona Press.

Burger, J., J. Brzorad, and M. Gochfeld. 1991. Immediate effects of an oil spill on behavior of fiddler crabs (Uca pugnax). Archives of Environmental Contamination and Toxicology 20(3):404-409.

Callander, S., J. Bolton, M.D. Jennions, and P.R.Y. Backwell. 2012. A farewell to arms: males with regenerated claws fight harder over resources. Animal Behaviour 84(3):619-622.

Callander, S., M.D. Jennions, and P.R.Y. Backwell. 2012. The effect of claw size and wave rate on female choice in a fiddler crab. Journal of Ethology 30(1):151-155.

Cammen, L.M., E.D. Seneca, and L.M. Stround. 1984. Long-term variation of fiddler crab populations in North Carolina salt marshes. Estuaries 7(2):171-175.

Christiansen, M.E., and W.T. Yang. 1976. Feeding experiments on the larvae of the fiddler crab Uca pugilator (Brachyura, Ocypodidae), reared in the laboratory. Aquaculture 8(1):91-98.

Christy, J.H. 1980. The Mating System of the Sand Fiddler Crab, Uca pugilator. Pp. 322 (Ithaca, NY: Cornell University).

Christy, J.H. 1982. Burrow structure and use in the sand fiddler crab Uca pugilator (Bosc). Animal Behaviour 30(3):687-694.

Clark, L.B. 1935. The visual acuity of the fiddler crab, Uca pugnax. Journal of General Physiology 19(2):311-319.

Crane, J. 1975. Fiddler Crabs of the World: Ocypodidae: Genus Uca Princeton, NJ: Princeton University Press.

Croll, G.A., and T.S. Klinger. 1994. Population structure, feeding and reproductive behavior, substratum selection, and predation of Uca pugnax and Uca pugilator in the marshes of Hunting Island, South Carolina. American Zoologist 34(5):53A.

Detto, T., M.D. Jennions, and P.R.Y. Backwell. 2010. When and why do territorial coalitions occur? Experimental evidence from a fiddler crab. American Naturalist 175(5):119-125.

Appendix 2 - Selection of Scholarly Articles

Eidietis, L., and M. Coffman. 2006. Crazy classroom critters: Using scientific inquiry in teacher education. Society for Integartive and Comparative Biology 2006 Annual Meeting.

Full, R.J., and C.F. Herreid, II. 1984. Fiddler crab exercise: The energetic cost of running sideways. Journal of Experimental Biology 109(1):141-161.

Genoni, G.P. 1991. Increased burrowing by fiddler crabs Uca rapax (Smith) (Decapoda: Ocypodidae) in response to low food supply. Journal of Experimental Marine Biology and Ecology 147(2):267-285.

Gosner, K.L. 1978. A Field Guide to the Atlantic Seashore from the Bay of Fundy to Cape Hatteras, Volume 24 Boston: Houghton Mifflin Company.

Guyselman, J.B. 1953. An analysis of the molting process in the fiddler crab, Uca pugilator. Biological Bulletin 104(2):115-137.

Hogarth, P.J. 2007. The Biology of Mangroves and Seagrasses New York: Oxford University Press.

Hopkins, P.M. 1982. Growth and regeneration patterns in the fiddler crab, Uca pugilator. Biological Bulletin 163(2):301-319.

Hopkins, P.M. 1993. Regeneration of walking legs in the fiddler crab Uca pugilator. American Zoologist 33(3):348-356.

Hyatt, G.W., and M. Salmon. 1979. Comparative statistical and information analysis of combat in fiddler crabs, Uca pugilator and U. pugnax. Behaviour 68:1-23.

Jaramillo, E., and K. Lunecke. 1988. The role of sediments in the distribution of Uca pugilator (Bosc) and Uca pugnax (Smith) (Crustacea, Brachyura) in a salt marsh of Cape Cod. Meeresforschung 32(1):46-52.

Jennions, M.D., P.R.Y. Backwell, M. Murai, and J.H. Christy. 2003. Hiding behaviour in fiddler crabs: How long should prey hide in response to a potential predator? Animal Behaviour 66(2):251-257.

Jensen, G.C. 1995. Pacific Coast Crabs and Shrimp Monterey, CA: Sea Challengers.

Kim, T.W., K. Sakamoto, Y. Henmi, and J.C. Choe. 2008. To court or not to court: reproductive decisions by male fiddler crabs in response to fluctuating food availability. Behavioral Ecology and Sociobiology 62(7):1139-1147.

Knott, D.M., E.L. Wenner, and P.H. Wendt. 1997. Effects of pipeline construction on the vegetation and macrofauna of two South Carolina, USA salt marshes. Wetlands 17(1):65-81.

Kraus, D.B. 1982. The burrow as a resource for reproduction and molting in the fiddler crab Uca minax. American Zoologist 22(4):869.

Appendix 2 - Selection of Scholarly Articles

Levinton, J.S., and M.L. Judge. 1993. The relationship of closing force to body size for the major claw of Uca pugnax (Decapoda: Ocypodidae). Functional Ecology 7(3):339-345.

Mantel, L.H., and R.S. Levin. 1973. Effects of multiple limb removal and stimulation on regeneration and molting in Uca pugilator. American Zoologist 13(4):1339.

McCarty, N.A., R.D. Roer, and R.B. Humm. 1985. Salinity preference behavior of the fiddler crab Uca minax. American Zoologist 25(4):37A.

McMahon, B.R., S. Morris, J.I. Spicer, and R.A. Byrne. 1990. Physiological responses to air exposure in the fiddler crab Uca pugilator. American Zoologist 30(4):61A.

Milner, R.N.C., I. Booksmythe, M.D. Jennions, and P.R.Y. Backwell. 2010. The battle of the sexes? Territory acquisition and defence in male and female fiddler crabs. Animal Behaviour 79(3):735-738.

Montague, C.L. 1980. A natural history of temperate western Atlantic fiddler crabs (genus Uca) with reference to their impact on the salt marsh. Contributions in Marine Science 23:25-55.

Palmer, J.D. 1990. The rhythmic lives of crabs. BioScience 40(5):352-358.

Appendix 2 - Selection of Scholarly Articles

Pope, D.S. 2000. Testing function of fiddler crab claw waving by manipulating social context. Behavioral Ecology and Sociobiology 47(6):432-437.

Powers, L.W. 1973. Ecological aspects of burrows and fiddler crab behavior. American Zoologist 13(4):1271

Pratt, A.E., and D.K. McLain. 2006. How dear is my enemy: Intruder-resident and resident-resident encounters in male sand fiddler crabs (Uca pugilator). Behaviour 143(5):597-617.

Pratt, A.E., D.K. McLain, and G.R. Lathrop. 2003. The assessment game in sand fiddler crab contests for breeding burrows. Animal Behaviour 65(5):945-955.

Rajkumar, P., S.M. Rollmann, T.A. Cook, and J.E. Layne. 2010. Molecular evidence for color discrimination in the Atlantic sand fiddler crab, Uca pugilator. Journal of Experimental Biology 213(24):4240-4248.

Ribeiro, P.D., J.H. Christy, R.J. Rissanen, and T.W. Kim. 2006. Males are attracted by their own courtship signals. Behavioral Ecology and Sociobiology 61(1):81-89.

Shock, B.C., C.M. Foran, and T.A. Stueckle. 2009. Effects of salinity stress on survival, metabolism, limb regeneration, and ecdysis in Uca pugnax. Journal of Crustacean Biology 29(3):293-301.

Appendix 2 - Selection of Scholarly Articles

Silbiger, N., and P. Munguia. 2008. Carapace color change in Uca pugilator as a response to temperature. Journal of Experimental Marine Biology and Ecology 355(1):41-46.

Weis, J.S. 1976. Effects of environmental factors on regeneration and molting in fiddler crabs. Biological Bulletin 150(1):152-162.

Glossary

A

acidity - The pH measurement judges the amount of acidity in water. It is an important measurement, but in terms of fiddler crab care, not as important as how much ammonia the water contains.

activated carbon - A carbon-based material used in some aquarium filters due to its highly absorbent qualities. Activated carbon will not remove either ammonia or nitrite from water, nor does is make the water "softer." It will, however, help to control any growth of organic material like algae.

air pump - An air pump is a device used by aquarists to ensure that the water in their tank is properly oxygenated to support life.

algae - This term refers to a broad number of aquatic plants that contain chlorophyll and tend to proliferate rapidly and in profusion in aquariums. Controlling algae growth is one of the nuisance tasks of aquarium care.

alkalinity - The measure of water's alkalinity is a rating of its capacity to neutralize acid without causing pH levels to fall. In simplistic terms, the more acid that can be added to water before the pH begins to drop, the greater the alkalinity or "buffering" capacity of the water.

Glossary

ammonia - Ammonia is the major toxin present in all tanks that represents a toxic hazard to the life forms contained therein. Ammonia builds up due to the presence of waste material in the water.

It's presence must be neutralized by the establishment of the nitrogen cycle in the tank, which introduces beneficial bacteria to consume the ammonia.

anoxia - A condition in which oxygen is completely absent from an environment.

aquaculture - The term used for the hobbyist or professional cultivation of aquatic animals in captivity.

aquascaping - In aquaculture, the process of selecting and arranging all the element of an aquarium to create the proper balance and bioload while maintain an aesthetically pleasing appearance is referred to as aquascaping.

aquarist - Any person who keeps an aquarium for pleasure or as a profession.

aquatic plant - Any plant that will grow fully or partially submerged in water.

B

beneficial bacteria - The bacteria that becomes established in an aquarium when the the nitrogen cycle is in place. The purpose of the bacteria is to convert harmful ammonia into less toxic nitrate.

benthic - Happening on or existing at the bottom of a body of water including an aquarium.

brackish - Slightly salty water present in places where fresh water sources meet the ocean, for instance estuaries. Fiddler crabs, although often sold as freshwater animals must have brackish water to survive.

C

carbonate hardness - An expression of the ability of water in your aquarium to absorb and neutralize acid.

carbon dioxide (CO_2) - A colorless, odorless gas created by animal respiration. Its presence in an aquarium must be countered by the use of an air filter to oxygenate the water.

chlorination - The process of adding chlorine to water as a purification agent to make it fit for human consumption. Water used in aquariums must be de-chlorinated or the tank inhabitants may sicken and die.

cycling - The process of establishing the nitrogen cycle in a tank to create the presence of beneficial bacteria to convert toxic ammonia to nitrates. If this cycle is not appropriately cultivated, the ammonia will reach toxic and fatal levels in short order.

D

detritus - Dead material (either bacterial, plant, or animal) that can be degraded or mineralized by bacterial process.

E

ecosystem - An interactive community of biological organisms and their physical environment.

estuary - The mouth of a river that meets the ocean, characterized by "brackish" or semi-saltwater.

F

fluorescent light - Aquarium lighting fixtures that provide a broad spectrum of light for a relatively low cost. This type of lighting is not required for fiddler crabs, although the creatures do enjoy both light and heat.

G

glass aquarium - Aquariums made of glass and produced in standard sizes. Routinely sold in pet stores. Customized and high volume tanks are made of acrylic.

H

hang on the back filter - A filter that sits on the outside and back of an aquarium. These units are outfitted with a draw

Glossary

tube that brings water into the mechanism for filtration and then channels it back into the tank.

heater - A device, usually a glass tube, connected to an electrical socket for the purpose of controlling water temperature in an aquarium. Usually accurate within 2 degrees.

hydrometer - An instrument used to measure the specific gravity of a fluid.

I

invertebrate - Animals that do not have a spine or backbone. Examples include starfish, clams, worms, and crags. It is not a good idea to attempt to house invertebrates with fiddler crabs.

N

nitrification - The bacteriological process by which ammonia is converted to nitrite, and then nitrite to nitrate. This is a crucial aspect of establishing the nitrogen cycle in a tank.

O

omnivore - An animal that eats both plant and animals as food.

P

predator - An animal that preys on other animals for food.

S

salinity - A measurement of dissolved salts in water.

specific gravity - A measurement of the amount of salt in aquarium water. Specific gravity is not a crucial measurement in tanks housing fiddler crabs only, but these crabs must have some degree of salt content to survive.

substrate - The material at the bottom of an aquarium, typically gravel or sand. Fiddler crabs must have a way to get out of the water, so typically enthusiasts build a sloping "beach" for their pets with fine aquarium or play sand.

T

territorial - Of or relating to a real or perceived sense of ownership of an area of the land, sea, or immediate environment. Fiddler crabs are highly territorial and can become aggressive in captivity if housed incorrectly.

W

water quality - A term referring to the chemical composition of water at any given time.

Index

Index

www.ingramcontent.com/pod-product-compliance
Lightning Source LLC
Chambersburg PA
CBHW072235290326
41934CB00008BA/1298